FALLING
BACK

FALLING
BACK

CHRISTINE EVANS

Poetry Wales Poets: 7

POETRY WALES PRESS
1986

POETRY WALES PRESS
56 PARCAU AVENUE, BRIDGEND, MID
GLAMORGAN

British Library Cataloguing in Publication Data

Evans, Christine
Falling Back : (the shepherd's widow). –
(Poetry Wales poets; 7)
I. Title
821'.914   PR6055.V14

ISBN 0-907476-63-5

Cover design: Jeane Rees

*The publisher acknowledges the financial support of
the Welsh Arts Council*

Typeset in Century Schoolbook
by Wordsmiths Ltd., Street
Printed by
D. Brown & Sons Ltd

Falling Back

(The Shepherd's Widow)

FOR HEATHER

If she could have wished, it would be
always winter. Empty skies
were easiest to live with
and no cold could really touch her now.
She looked full face into the sun;
some mornings, it got down at her level
puffing a little, to peer myopically

at her through the trees. The first weeks
after her sister went back home she sat
still as driftwood, the taste of muteness
thick in her mouth. Night after night
she wheeled him urgently past white-tiled walls
or watched his endless falling
into depths that would not let her follow

his eyes wide open till
the shock-waves woke her, wet with sweat and
   shuddering
for breath. And there were other dreams
in which she found it was not him at all
in the coffin she had just seen covered
with cold earth. Then all next day
there was a gnawing at the dull sponge of her
   brain.

She knew the neighbours whispered,
were concerned, but could not bear
to be for long with anyone. The dogs' eyes,
even, offered her too much: she'd asked
Huw's friends to take them, unable to decide
which to sell or keep or have put down.
In the yard now only dead leaves stirred.

7

It was a quiet place, set high, towards the hill.
Days on end, she saw no-one, could not set foot
outside, for even to get fuel or food
from the deep freeze felt like an exposure
that might dissolve all her defences
and reveal her shapeless, squirming,
helpless as an unhoused snail.

People did call – for politeness' sake,
she felt – but even friends were met
with some excuse at the front door,
her face clearing as she closed it
against the questions that they could not ask,
the sympathy they'd wrapped up, clumsily,
to offer if they could get near enough.

Draughts caught at her skin, and daylight nudged,
so for weeks she kept doors shut and curtains
closed: air in all the rooms
that used to take its flavour from the wind,
the sun-dried linen and warm bread,
was stale and trapped; chilled like fog.
But she, who'd always felt the cold,

no longer noticed. Since the funeral,
she lived a blur
as if all the windows of her mind were streaming
with all the tears that had not fallen
from her eyes, cocooning her
as the landscape of the year was ripped apart
its fading fragments whirled and scattered,

cold as ash. Occasionally,
out of habit, she picked up a book
or turned the telly on; even, sometimes, sat down
to look at it, letting the words
fluff up in her head like cotton wool,
the pictures flicker over her
inscrutable as lightning. Around her

flotsam of an older life
was left to lie: not just his things,
but all that she'd been busy with
on the eleventh of October. Jars washed for jam
stranded on the draining board, shopping lists,
a pumpkin oozing into sticky sweetness,
were pointers to the purpose of those moments

before she heard the news. Now, from leaf-fall
through first frosts, she was a shrivelled presence,
sitting it out. Slow dust settled
where it fell. The green and flowering plants
she'd grown from seed and tended daily
dried up; turned brown; were stark black fingers
outlined on the sills at dawn

when she had bothered
not to leave lights on. Time too
had slipped the paragraphs
that made its meaning small enough.
She slept just when she could, downstairs,
and often in her clothes; ate
in handfuls, standing up, at any hour

of day or night. And whenever she lay down
she clutched the jumper he had worn on that
   last day,
the dark blue Aran she'd just finished.
It kept his smell; was warmth
for her to curl round. The closest she could
   ever come
to flesh that would no longer flinch
from freezing or from spring.

Among the ruins, intermittently,
a sense of self surprised her: physically,
she moved on, while her mind sat still, a passenger,
amazed how often she must cut
her toe- and finger-nails, how, suddenly,
her hair was long; and how, punctually, painlessly,
her body bled, keeping its options open.

It was as such landmarks slipped behind
that she began to panic at the thought
of winter's passing. In the pitiless bright days
of autumn she'd accepted everything
they'd told her, signed at every
pencilled cross; accepted, after Lady Day,
the shepherd's cottage must be empty.

This knowledge, like an indicator light
winking urgently among a mass of instruments
she could not understand, made her feel
outside the airlock of her dullness
the universe was dizzy as she plunged,
with no course plotted, stabilisers gone,
ever outwards, backwards, falling out of range.

And then her mouth was dry
or full of sourness that she fought back down
with anger. Why should it be she
left suddenly alone to take control
with no hand on her arm, no last approving word?
Why had he never thought of this,
building a life that needed

no-one else, a world of quiet places
where she had lost the trick of being strong?
She was so savage with her memories
she felt resentment shake
her, worse than grief, and fear of greater loss
curled her like a child in pain,
clinging blindly to the dying year,

hugging a pretence: he was still there,
might soon come home for dinner
or nip in to phone the boss. Strange, to miss
the mopping-up of muddy prints.
But as the days contracted sharply
it was easier keeping hopelessness
at bay: as she sat on in the dark

there was, sometimes, awareness
in the unstirred air – or was it in herself? –
a moving warmth that grew, unfolding
into recognition, an absolute
she could relax into. To belong
not just with him, but with a vast dark unity
she had never glimpsed before.

There was no thought of how
or what in her response, only welcoming
a sense of contact that had budded first
driving from the hospital
when there was finally no hope,
no heartbeat left. The sky was bleached with dawn;
she had watched birds falling through the
    empty air

waiting for some pain, but felt instead
a last pulse of his consciousness
reaching out to reassure her.
A warmth quiet as a sunset,
close as breath, had touched her then
spread through and stayed throughout the
    wretched dark
until weeks of wordlessness

had tuned her senses. Now she rode
moments of sureness that she would survive,
even elation: she was herself once more,
and whole. What else could ever hurt?
She need no longer shut herself away, laired
like a sick animal. She would look out again
when daylight seeped back through the hills.

At Christmas, the telephone
began to ring again, but though she felt like
    healing,
now she did not want layers of events
burying his presence; to be distracted
by voices, faces, obligations,
blurring a focus that began to wake
delight in detail he had shown her first –

12

that she could lose herself in looking.
In that cold clearness, stripped bare,
the shapes of things seemed much more
than themselves: seed heads against an evening sky
like fire; patterns in the ice;
one patch of blue among the cumulus
brief and delicate as flowers;

and the view across the valley, its small wood,
with meaning for her that had grown
through season shared. Now it was more than
    seeing
the colours on the hillside change
and coarsen, like a sick beast's hide;
there was a message she could almost read
in the great slow gestures of the trees.

In the dead of the year, she dreamed
he brought her bilberries
and a single garden rose they had once seen
forcing its way through brambles
in a rectangle of stones
high on the slopes of the Carneddau.
Something usually survives, he'd said.

For a few nights then, she slept
without the Mogadon, letting herself go
as blackness in enormous, dreamless surges
washed over her. The phone rang
like an aching tooth, how long, how many times,
she did not count, but it had given up
when the barren rhythm of her widowed nights

clamped down. She started out of bed
in terror that a voice had called
her name, and she had missed him,
or woke to find her breasts were full
of aching, as if the baby of their early marriage
had even yet not faded out of life. Found only
    silence
thick on her face, or the empty raging of the
    wind,

but rousing once when it had quietened,
going north, she sat up to watch
the moon and stars. Her arms, the room,
were streaming with white light, and stillness
so intense it was like singing
gripped the hills. All other human eyes
were shut against the sight: it was hers.

But woke stiffly, to a sunrise
like a leaking wound. All day, cold rain,
with slivers of ice dropped sullenly
from the eye of the wind, and birds still waiting,
mourning ragged bundles blown about
outside the kitchen window. Dully
she thought, they are victims too,

and with anger's inspiration, saw
it should not be so, was something due
to her, and snatching up what she could find –
suet, cream crackers soggy in the tin,
packets of cereal she did not eat –
at last she could not fail to see
mouse dirt, black mould, the litter of decay.

14

Cobwebs trawled the dresser shelves
and the silver cups he'd won at trials
were dull as outgrown memories. Dust
traced the names on them – 'Jess', 'Roy', 'Glen'.
Remembering Stanraer, the rain in Kendal
when Jess was still a pup, and how he smiled
    with pleasure
at the younger man who won last year,

she wiped them clean, and watched warm drops
fall on her hands. Luxurious as rain in summer
tears came at last, easing out this storm
with gentleness; lending her the strength
to sweep and scrub and carry out
the debris. Each job she finished was a knot
in her unravelling; a toehold

for the long climb back. Outside were more
reproaches: the garden lay awash
with weeds; blackened hulks and spars of summer
sprawled. He left the last potatoes
to be lifted and the ritual digging-in
until those easy autumn weeks
when all the sales were over and the rams

back on the mountain, the real beginning
of the sheep man's year. Sodden drifts of leaves
had clogged the drains and gutters.
Cowshed and barn were sour
with greying straw and last year's bales
falling apart. No more logs, neatly stacked
with kindling separate, for her ease.

Between the trees, already there was twilight
clotting round the roots and tangling in brambles,
a faint smoke rising from the heaps
of ruined growth she scuffled. Only moss
was still a gleaming green. Almost luminous,
fungus trickling down the thicker trunks
glistened, nudging on the night's approach.

The air was heavy with decay
and wet logs lay inert as corpses.
There was not one that she could shift.
This time, her tears were helpless,
weakening. She dashed them angrily
away, crying aloud for him
to help her if she had to keep on trying –

but no warmth came, the silent trees stood round
aloof, and for a moment, shamed,
she saw her petulance in their perspective.
Beech and oak could not give up – the sap
was rising still and rippling outwards
from the toughening heart. Endure
or strive: there was no other option.

Half-blindly she reached out a hand
to the closest trunk, and in a gesture
of kinship, of apology, she clasped it
with both arms and closed her eyes
to share its strength. The bark against her cheek
was cold but smooth with rain, that washed
    away
the taste of tears. She sensed how deep,

how far, its roots must spread
and then grew conscious of another time scale,
and below that yet another, as the leaves and
    rotting wood
were broken down again to soil
to grow new oaks, and as the rocks themselves
heaved and shifted in a giant sleep
that made death seem a breathing space.

Next morning, she went back with saw and axe,
surprised to find a core of challenge
growing in her. Working in that patient air,
tiring her body, helped
her waking hours get back
in kilter. She began to eat again
although at first the smell of cooking

with its taint of grease could turn her sick
as she came in from the frosty woods
or shopping in the village, where she spoke
of weather forecasts or the price of barrens
as though they mattered. Grateful
for the questions bitten back, assured her
    neighbours
she was able to keep busy; at least, was out

as long as daylight lasted,
shaking off the closeness
of those walls that were her comfort once,
the only way
to hold the old shape of her life. Now
the house was a sad husk; she heard it
rattling round her in the small hours

and waited, wide-eyed, for the morning
for the freedom of the high clear places
she was rediscovering, walking on the folded tops
till there was nothing but the rhythm
of her striding and the wash of air
over her face. In a world clenched hard
against the cold, she was chaff, was spindrift

translucent as the countries in the sky
that beckoned, prophesied
and moved on. She left no trace
in the bracken-ash, the stripped black wires
of heather or sealed-in stream. But all the time
the spring that she could not ignore
was groping nearer on the tilting earth

stirring small song in the blackthorn, whorls
of tender green despite the crystals
that crusted the leaf-mould
even at noon. A bulling heifer in the valley
drooled and blared her readiness to breed
hour after hour, and close in the dark
before dawn a vixen gasped and screamed.

Weeks sharpening the year, before the ice
gave way. She woke to quilted silence
and a sense of expectation, a surprise prepared.
The only thing that seemed to move
her hand in the curtain's colours; but tracks
deliberate dark letters
skirted her garden, a shepherd's whistles
    reached her

like the call of some exotic bird
stranded in the vagueness. That day at dusk
small groups of sheep began to drift downhill
to where Huw would have fed them
in hard weather. She watched them
from the empty shadows
of her kitchen. The ewes were heavy now;

most she recognised and one or two,
old friends that she had bottle fed,
called plaintively. At last, reluctant,
she pulled on boots and anorak
to take out what was left
of last year's hay and barley. Hemmed in by
    their jostling
snow-matted backs, the clouds of their breath

hot through her gloves, she was reminded
the new life unfolding in them strongly now
would be the end of all his years of work,
the five-month total of the busy days
before his death. Perhaps it would not have
    been enough,
the few fields he'd been saving for,
the hand-picked flock, dogs to train.

Out of old habit, she swung the torchlight round
to check for sickening ewes
lying alone. The glowing greenish eyes
made scattered constellations in the beam;
they gave her, suddenly, a sense of leaving
like seeing that the train
is gently pulling out, the boat no longer

secured to the jetty. She would not
do this again, whatever else
became of her. And there it was –
a future unimaginably empty, vague
yet imminent as fog. How could she plan
her own uprooting? What hope
in anything she built? She was forty-six years old,

unqualified, inept, and on the downward slope.
Panicky and half-formed thoughts
swirled round her, like the blurring flakes
the sky was letting go again.
She was, completely, on her own; would never
have his warmth to curl against,
the slow comfort of his voice. Who was she

then, without him, without the quarter century
she had to throw away? The youngest child
(most loved, the others used to tell her)
of parents who had named her
Hilary, *for laughter*, rounded to Eleri
in the soft Welsh vowels
of the grandmother they had come home to

and the salt world of the schoolyard on the hill,
so that now she shrank from the assertion
of her official name on cheques, at polling stations.
For the three days she was islanded
in the wide stare of the snow,
she sought to find some solid ground,
to recall some other times

when she had stood alone. The fighting shy
of adolescence did not count:
endless evenings in the furnished room
or the grubby flat shared later
so clearly only temporary
they were a game or an initiation.
Married, the only nights they slept apart

were when she was in hospital –
the baby; tests; at last, the operation.
That long dry summer, she backed off, aloof,
clenched in her cave of self until her husband
seemed smaller to her than the surgeons.
But tending her weakness, waking to relief
   together,
had laced old dependence even surer.

It seemed now she had always played
for safety – the choices hardly made
but left to harden round her. So, not the art course
urged by her teachers, but a job
an uncle found her with a country vet;
not the boys on motorbikes, but a man
already seasoned snagged her gaze.

She felt his strength firm-rooted, like a tree,
and yet his hands were gentle
round the injured cat he had brought in.
Walking with him on the hill
she recognised the confident long pace
of a man accustomed to steep places,
a dream of distance in the clear blue eyes

roused easily to eagerness or laughter.
There had been friends: mostly, couples
who, with children to talk over,
began to show some pity or unease
before they dropped away. Then, moving house
with each new job, settling in Gwynedd,
they lost the habit of exchange.

In the cocoon they had made together
what she had become was his –
so what of him? What buds of possibility
had she, by her presence, smothered,
or had he, reflecting all she seemed to need,
drawn confidence she had not known
was hers to tender?

Through the dark months dreams
of lovemaking had flooded her
only with horror: lip on lip and murmuring
or as he leant down to her breasts, his hair
fine as hill grass against her throat,
she'd felt the old stained dressings of his skin
begin to flake and slime and fall away

but on that third slow-moving ghost-faced night
found herself sprawling in a strange wild garden
pulling down the thick green stalks
about her face until the air was dancing
in a haze of sunlit pollen, every grain
a microscopic enclosed world
responding to no accidental tune

shaken in the small hours by the memory
of the smooth-skinned naked summer they could
   make
in any season, the big bones of his thighs
masts for hers to cling to, breath
the song of breakers
that they rode. Waking with his touch
still on her hair, wealth

she did not fight to keep, began to hear
a shuffle, an irregular slow drip
that spelt a thaw, and by dinner time,
the pasture only streaked with white,
one ewe too still beside the stream
was plain. Not lambing: nowhere near,
but crow-bait, blind and trembling

with what Huw would call clwy'r eira,
the snow sickness – twin lambs inside her
leaching energy much faster
that the liver broke it down until, brain- starved,
the sheep would never eat again. Shelter
and stilboestrol might be in time:
nothing she could do alone.

All winter, she had avoided meeting
the new man. Now, trudged two miles
through wood and fields (the road still blocked)
to a morass of sludge and melting snow
that was the farmyard. Three miserable sheepdogs
barked and rattled at the limit of their chains
and with a gust of steam and frying chips

the caravan door swung wide
and she was welcomed in, wet boots and all,
by a girl who could have been her daughter,
dishcloth in hand, a child, big-eyed, with wispy hair,
clinging to her legs but holding out his toys
as they drank tea. A small ecstatic terrier bitch
jumped up, escaping her five pups

that growled and tumbled, chewing at their socks
breaking up the talk that only touched on sheep:
where to buy yeast, the baby due in June,
neighbours and plants and buses into town. Leaving,
she bent to move the puppy flopped asleep
across her feet and held it for a moment,
responding to its warmth and clean young smell.

It moaned and nuzzled in against her hand.
Through folds of milk-fat flesh and fluff
she traced the intricate tenacity
of bone; and with an impulse like salvation
found herself agreeing she would take this one
in three weeks' time. That night, she slept
as if she'd worked all day.

Green follows snow. Her sister wrote
from Cheltenham, of wallpaper and daffodils, a trip
to Germany at Easter to prepare
Julie for her O levels. And how she must
feel free to come and stay, at any time.
Please let them know her new address.
The letter ended 'with much love'.

And all at once the ewes on lower ground
began to lamb, returning as the birds would
to old nest-sites. The pattern of the years
stretched out implacable as snowfall,
perhaps as merciful, but she could not
so abruptly face the burying
of all her tracks. Fled in panic to the coast

but there was no comfort there.
The sea lay sullen as used metal
with a tight steel rim at the horizon
like the arcus in the eyes
of strong old women, a sort of scarring
in the grain. Driving home
past blackthorn thickening with bloom

as a last frost and catkins that began
their beckoning, she found her mind was full
of ancestors. All evening she scanned
the faces in old photographs.
For the camera at least
they did not look bereft; but strong, contained,
as if they knew they could take grief

within their stride. Like zoo-bred apes with young,
she thought, we have not learnt to handle
death. At ten this grandmother had to take
a stillborn sibling in a cardboard box
for pauper's burial; watch Edith, eight years older,
coughing blood and sweating
in the bed the sisters shared. Later saw

three sons, the young men of a generation,
shipped off to France. She had survived
far more than she could tell of; yet,
from the stiff board of the Edwardian family group
to the Instamatic on the lawn
outside the geriatric ward
she gazed, unflinching, straight ahead.

Nothing so delicate as pleasure
showed, although it surely flowered
in the leafy summer evenings of her youth
or berrying with her babies by the river
when time flowed like a shining tune
within the blackbird's song. She looked
as if she would agree, but, tightlipped, add:

– *And paid for.* Damp fogged the mirror,
made the living image more remote
than the old photograph's; Eleri must lean close
to see new sharpness in her cheeks and at her chin;
that though her eyes were dull
as rainwashed bark, they held a strength
that could be richer than resilience.

Versions of her face: how few known,
not even her own father in his khaki.
More uniforms: uncles stiff with self- importance,
reminding her of geese that have survived
another Christmas. But their women, growing
    brittle,
stared out the ironies of time
with no betraying hope or pain or fear.

Some of them perhaps were waiting to float free.
With hindsight, their harrowing
brought home how clean her hurt had been:
whatever happened had been by his will, his
exercise of skill, a chance
of his own stepping. The death with dignity
he said each animal deserved.

She had always told herself that worse
was borne by others, faced an older self
but for the first time suddenly
she felt the truth of it and pity
like an indrawn breath of pain
possessed her, a swell of feeling
breaking free and making new connections.

She sat on in the ebbing firelight
half-aware that she was cramped and cold,
of the high thin cries of young lambs waking
for the first time in the dark alone,
and was lifted by a sense of kinship;
that she was linked by more than she could know
beyond the groove her own life followed

and compassion swept her, strong enough
to embrace herself so she could finally accept
the barrenness of hoarding
joy once had, to watch it wither
as an apple will round its own sweetness
till only the smell of it is left
in a tainted room.

When, stiffly, she got up, the shadows moved
deep in the window, as though she could have been
companioned by the other selves
she conjured; but there was no-one else,
she knew, no other warmth but hers
to call on. The clock Huw's father made
ticked towards another century

as it would go on doing at the heart
of this still night-shrouded winter home
where it belonged. She would let the girl
inherit; cleared, she might discover
aspects of herself to knit and grow
like the white scars of a well-laid hedge.
Find why her life had gone on mattering.

And so at last the ending season brought her
to the place her mind had most avoided –
the derelict slate workings where he'd lain
all dry bright autumn afternoon
after the fall. She had thought to face some
    horror here,
and there was death enough
among the heaps of spoil and in the huts

where sheep had crept at last into the dark –
but with no more loss in it
than in water draining back to join the tide
and spin again in sunlit foam
before the next wave breaks. Rowans
sprouted through layers of dull slate
and saxifrage, with moss and stonecrop, leapt

chasms to find a fingerhold of soil.
Growth was softening all the jagged edges
and underneath the numbness
life ran still, the chance of eagerness
she knew that he, who mourned
each stillborn lamb, would want to quicken
in her too. On rising air above the ravens' nest

she let the old life go, looking south clear-eyed
as sunset turned the distant lakes to ink.
This year she would not witness, more than he,
how blossom overflowed the pits with sweetness
of hawthorn, crabapple, wild cherry;
how wood-anemone and early violet might show
just where his warmth had leaked into the earth.

She sat so still that five last ewes
tapping uphill deliberate as the blind
were unaware, and shadows sidled up
to settle round her. There would be packing,
preparations, more advertisements to find;
to answer. But she had learned her ground. Soon,
would step out surely, though there were no stars.